A WRITER'S SKETCH

AN ORIGINAL BOOK OF POEMS WRITTEN BY

RONALD W. SCHULMAN

ARTWORK BY

MIRIAM SCHULMAN

A WRITER'S SKETCH

An original book of poems written by Ronald W. Schulman.

All original artwork by Miriam Schulman.

Book design and layout by Anna Kuhlmey.

Edited by Talia Schulman.

DEDICATION

Writing is a lifetime proposition. We learn many things as we mature through the chapters of our life and experience the world—near and far. The following influences guide me along the way with writing and moreover, focusing on the world for its beauty as well as the shortcomings. I believe, as do millions of others, that we need to leave the world in better working order than we found it.

First, my high school English teacher at Jeff-Youngsville High School, Edna Clark (who recently passed away) taught us to appreciate the poets and great novelists, to express ourselves and to be writers right from the start. She made us buy blank journals (which she called "nothing books") and we became our own authors at the ripe age of 16-17 years old. Our written expression became our poetry, essays, short stories and short novels.
This experience catapulted my writing career 40 years ago.

Professional authors and musicians influence me over the years, but I can't put my finger on just one or two people so let me batch together this list: Ralph Waldo Emerson, Sinclair Lewis, Somerset Maugham, Ernest Hemingway, Philip Roth, James Baldwin, Bob Dylan, George Harrison, Paul Simon, and the Moody Blues. I appreciate authors, poets and musicians who address the human condition clearly, make us think, describe a scene, and tell a true to life story that allows us to experience what I call "convincing cause" and not "crummy clutter."

I am inspired by my family and friends as well as business associates. I love to learn and retain the knowledge in a vault where I draw from; it helps me decipher better ways to improve the world from the steps that I take and let this learning be my road map. Cumulative learning is so important in our lives. We need to build on everything that we experience and as we write more and more, the results should be more keen, sharp and effective. More in focus.

Finally, I thank my wife, Miriam, my daughter, Talia and my son, Seth, for always being an inspiration for me and for providing lots of love, laughter, and support. We have a great time together and we always enjoy telling each other stories, jokes, accomplishments and discussing important issues of the day. I love you.

DOWNLOAD THE FREE AUDIOBOOK!

READ THIS FIRST

Just to say thanks for buying my book, I would like to give you the audiobook version 100% free.

TO DOWNLOAD GO TO:

schulmanart.com/audiopoems

CHAPTERS

ACKNOWLEDGEMENTS

I would like to express my deep gratitude to the family and friends in the official *A Writer's Sketch* book launch team who helped make this book release possible:

- Rita Carbuhn -
- Karen Rushton -
- Sharon Skolnik -
- Deborah Strek -
- Deb Lund -
- Blanca Ramirez -
- Jane Silverman -
- Ruthann Baler -

I set out to write—a nearly 17-year-old boy with a pen, notebook, bursting ideas and many roads to follow. Did the 17-year-old boy in me know how much the world would change and how much it wouldn't? I think that I did. I had good intuition and instinct—as seasoned as a detective on the trail. And not a cold trail. It was a hot trail back then, a trail that I needed to pursue for a long time. But how long is long? Is 40 years a long time? I don't think so. I still have good leads to follow and many more poetry trails to explore.

The story starts in late 1979 from my bedroom in Jeffersonville, NY—a small upstate New York town in the Catskill Mountains—as I look out my window at the row of mature trees behind our house, which border a babbling brook. I see the brook's cold fall waters, swelling the banks, challenging the rocks, moving sticks, branches and leaves out of the way, making a mad dash downstream. The brook's water was always very cold. And so was the fall air; it woke you up with one inhalation. It was a great time to be a kid and a budding writer.

It was also a great time to practice my baseball swing with an old beaten-up wood bat. I would hit a pile of rocks as far as I could into the woods— right-handed and lefty too. This was my off-season batting practice: tossing a rock up and then smashing it as far as I could. That 17-year-old wanted to play third base for the Yankees, a dream thousands of kids have. Pushing sports' dreams aside, I often looked out the window and said to myself that I had a lot to give and offer to this world. Did I know what I was going to give, where to go, and what exactly I would do? Who would I help? Did I have a hunch that I was leaving there for somewhere new and somewhere altogether different?

The trail that I set out—knowingly or not—back in 1979 is what I have followed since then. It is my life map and a story to tell. And this story is seen through my eyes, which always look at the world in wonder and amazement and at other times, ripe with ideas to improve what we need to change. Change for the better and change for all, not just change for the select few. This life map serves me well as I have helped to build thousands of affordable housing units during the past 35 years.

The ideas and roads that I have followed over the years are indeed many. You will see a lot in this book—woven through my eyes in different years and in different places with maturing vantage points—maturing prose. These pieces focus on objects, people, places, dreams, thoughts, and especially hopes.

I can still feel the cold air coming through that bedroom window on a cool spring or fall day—slapping me in the face, waking me up. The memory brings me back when I need to return to my original writing roots, my original questions. As I look at the world four decades later, now a middle-aged adult with two grown children who are both older than that 17 year old boy in me, I can't believe how much time has gone by and some critical changes that I wrote about years ago still need to be made in this world.

Back then, I was old for my age. I was old for the desire to change the world and old to know that we need to do good things to survive and thrive.

Today, that young maturity reminds me of a refrain lyric in Bob Dylan's "My Back Pages," "Oh, but I was so much older then; I'm younger than that now." I think that we all should get younger as life goes on, just to keep it interesting, fresh and new.

Through the past 40 years, I have composed my thoughts into various forms of poetry and prose. These passages are addressed to loved ones, people, society and the world at large. I present them in this book as original as possible for I want to represent the time in which they are written—literary photographs of place, purpose and my mind's view at the time.

Our minds meander a lot in our lives, but we seem to come back to an original road. It's the road that we start to walk down in our early maturing years. We all may take forks, twists and turns, and yet we nearly always come back to one main road—it's our individual path to pursue fueled by our true life purpose.

Here are several pages of my mind. Enjoy and engage your own mind. *Think of your own road.* Relate and create poetry, your own purpose and conclusions—perhaps your own solutions. That's how our minds work best...we think, construct, make our marks and then connect the dots in our lives.

RWS
07.09.2019

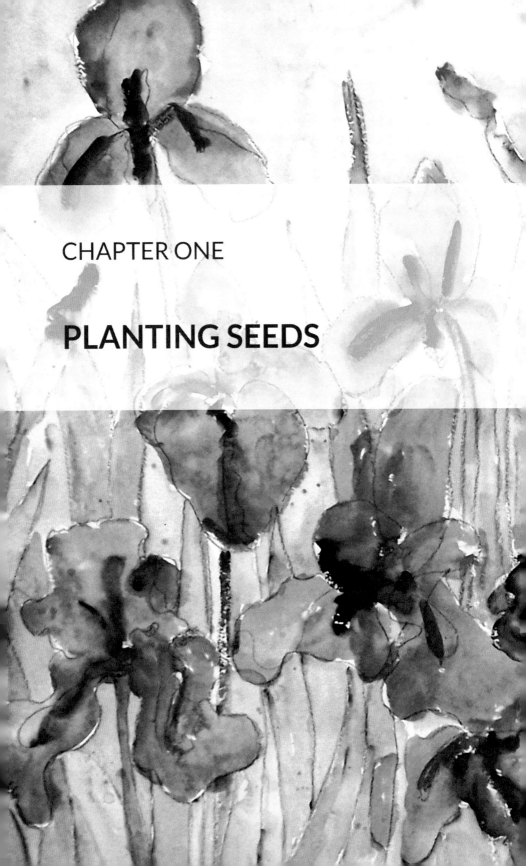

CHAPTER ONE

PLANTING SEEDS

TIN ROOF RAIN

White skies envelope me
between the flaps
of glued—down good.
Stuck together, I filter grand ideas
through the mechanics of
my mind.

Sounds echo through
my ears
like a tin roof rain.
And some voices are heard,
though they remain
soft and sketchy.

Problems present
thoughts and choices
to be understood.
Yet, I believe that I can fend off
ornery obstacles
from the right side of my brain.

My head lifts
and joins my psyche
in claiming the days
which remain.
And delicately do so
while I start to dance down the road.

RWS
6.16.1981

CIRRUS CLOUDS

I listened to Neil Young
while three flies pestered me.
It was during "Expecting to Fly,"
when I imagined that I would like to be
in the perfect realm that I have planned
for all the people like me
wherever they may be living, like me.

I've got to get away
from all of the hassles.
They're dragging me down—
lower than I'd like to be.
It's sure gonna take
a lot of time.
Yeah,
time takes so damn long.

So you want to live
to help others
and live to give yourself to someone?
Then why don't I do it?
Why do I live
like vanishing cirrus clouds?
Floating behind curtains.

I do have some good ideas.
I think as good
as others. Pretty good in fact.
Hey, I hear that John Lennon is making a new album,
which should be out soon.
I hope so.
It's been a long time.

RWS
8.23.1980

PLANT MY GARDEN

Rise from the ground floor, to the highest
floor known
where you can meet your place in the world.
Reshape things as they are
into beliefs that you hold and value.
Put a very high price on success
and never give in to just being there.
Strive for more than most.
Not at the cost of most.
But at your and their benefit.
This formula works
because you have tested it.
You're long out of the laboratory.

Success and sincerity deliver these goods.
Ones who flaunt fail in the long run and who
wants that to happen?
I would rather make the slow, sure climb
and stick a firm stake in my own mountain.
Plant it purely.
Plant my garden of success,
tend to it and make it grow.
Let the sun do its work and feel the warmth
from above.
It's simple.
Follow this road for good.
Watch me rise.

RWS
12.23.2013

HARVESTING

Sense that it is all coming together,
in a great big wonderful way.
The way when you won a baseball game
or had a great five—mile run.
It's where all the parts are in sync and
the sum correctly adds up.

Believe it when you feel it.
The time is here.
You are the creator and the inventor of things—feelings and successes.
It's like a story that you've heard before.
The glossy magazine story that you sometimes see in the racks …
you're now in it.

Take this in, reap the goodness and the grandeur.
You have become a part
of the successful inner workings.
And you are its master mechanic, its leader
and now its major benefactor.
It's like harvesting rich crops in the most perfect fall.

Move forward with this plan and also chart new courses.
Don't leave a rock unturned.
Make it better because every day is the foundation for the next.
Believe in ever growing dreams, which become your new reality.
You are wise to give thanks. Go forward anew.
Harvesting...

RWS
8.01.2013

CHAPTER TWO

THOUGHTS FOR SALE

SKY LIFE

As I look out my bedroom window, I see
wonderment.
Intricate patterns.
The sky is so full of life.
There is an ocean of imaginative thought out
there.
Dark shades of blue outline the light blues.
The naked trees sway endlessly while they
stare back at me.
Over the mountains,
the fading rays of the sun end another day of
work.
As every minute passes, the sky grows darker
and darker until
I can no longer gaze at the mystical patterns—
for they have turned
their backs to me.

RWS
1.08.1980

THOUGHTS FOR SALE

I sit
with my mind
wide open
to wide—open
thoughts.

The night's midst
and a bright light
warm the silence,
coaxing wide—open
words to hit the paper.

And in this calm
inspiration abounds
and my wide—open thoughts
quietly reach
fruition.

These are not
any old thoughts,
they are wide—open thoughts.
Moreover, they are
thoughts for sale.

RWS
12.01.1979

TRANQUILITY

Smooth,
endless motions.
There is no set rhythm.
Simple stems of grass blowing
express this beautiful word.

Tranquility
is precious
to those whose minds
are capable of being
tranquil.

RWS
1.16.1980

ANOTHER REFLECTION

Another trail,
one more humble outing,
which all too plainly
presents old facets and fables.

Slithering away,
you feel conviction
might raise its ugly head
and take another prisoner or two.

You trace
slushy footprints
which look all too friendly,
but you keep walking.

Inching forward,
you know that
your knee—jerkisms
will steer you clear yet again.

You then look
around to see
another reflection
of the same image.

RWS
7.26.1988

LONG TIME STRUCTURE

Trapped in a circle, the frozen radii.
Stretching to demand
in an arc's way or a fulcrum's command.
Nothing drawn,
only a maze
of silent stands.

Desired motion
struck to a stop
by an inset mechanism of who knows what.
Tired, thirsting for anew,
begging for a plan, scheme,
maybe two.

Linked in a row, the solid segments.
Gasping to glitter
in the broken line's way or a comic's deliver.
It's too bad that the land remains unsowed,
amidst the pencil
and what we know.

RWS
3.01.1984

STRINGS & NOTES

Notes surround the room,
enveloping the air and soothing
the souls.
The score
pumps us back to
life.

The arrangement of
strings and notes.
Pitch that is
perfect
saves us in this room
and sends us to the moon.

Hear it
dance in your brain,
the best way that
a tone tunes us up,
surrounding
everyone.

Resolved that we
are recreated,
melted
into a whole being again.
Time is
perfect.

Remember the next time
that we recoil
into disturbance,
notes are near and they are pure
and it is all so very
perfect.

RWS
5.09.2013

HINT OF HONEY

Bright as a light that shines on your hand
as you open the summer screen door
in the hot Sunday morning sun, when you step
out
to sit on a favorite porch chair
and dream.
About not much at all
since it is a Sunday.
After all.

Energy comes from within this light and wraps
around
its surroundings in pure warmth,
the type that soothes you and makes you
forget time and just enjoy
the state of being.
It happens to take place before
your eyes.
On a private stage.

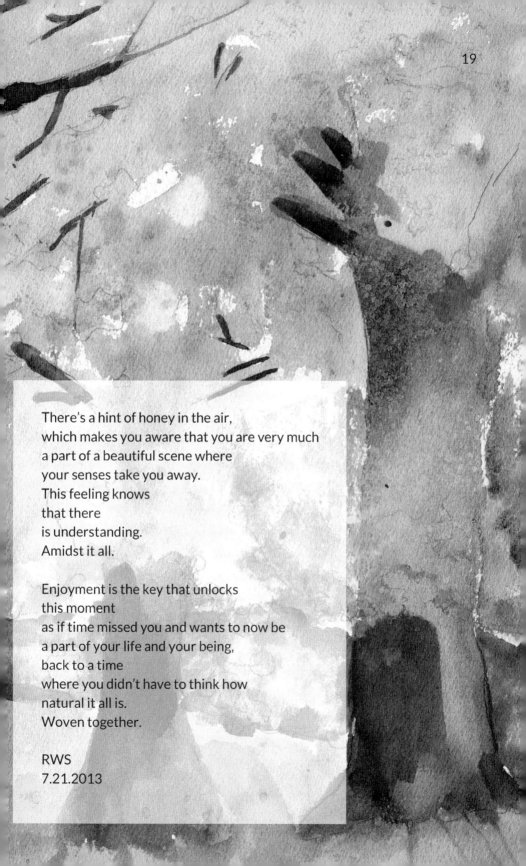

There's a hint of honey in the air,
which makes you aware that you are very much
a part of a beautiful scene where
your senses take you away.
This feeling knows
that there
is understanding.
Amidst it all.

Enjoyment is the key that unlocks
this moment
as if time missed you and wants to now be
a part of your life and your being,
back to a time
where you didn't have to think how
natural it all is.
Woven together.

RWS
7.21.2013

CHAPTER THREE

NEW YORK CITY

CITYSCAPE

Steel silos challenge
the feathered ones.
If only they could climb
to the top,
they would.

Whispers, cries
and shrills.
Voices bestow their call.
But answers
are seldom heard.

Engines allow movement
be an unending state.
Sirens yelp.
Children shed tears.
Couples clutch tight.

Humans race throughout
defined areas.
They stack
themselves into
unpleasant quarters.

And I look up and down.
In and out.
But I only find
a predictable
eternity.

RWS
6.19.1985

SIXTH AVENUE

Innocent
interlude
so well
intended.

It crushes
one's spirit
when splintered
to hell.

Yeah,
I've heard that
a tango's
for two.

But why not
rumba alone
and avoid swollen sighs
and sweltering sages?

RWS
4.5.1988

GULLS ON THE ROOF

Those grey coats
who sit
in brown pools.
They yield curious contempt.

Amidst cracked rows
of white bricks
they gaze down
at the roaring alleys of humanity.

They chat
and contemplate
the day's deeds.
They enjoy quiet moments.

One head sways
back and forth.
Two shoulders stretch—
determined to succeed.

They turn to me
and stare me down—
eye to eye.
And then they wink!

I cautiously nod.
They smile and chuckle.
Having made someone else's day.
They then turn away.

RWS
6.11.1985

TRADING ZONES

Show me your wares on Kenmare,
your dusty tunes on Broome,
your five-n-dime fancies on Delancey,
your chicken stew pots on Mott,
and your used dowry on Bowery.

I'll give you the time to be sublime,
the ways and means to be so keen,
the trails and scores that say "pay some more,"
the bleeding hearts that reek of cupid's darts,
and the chilling tears in shot of a child's ear.

RWS
6.10.1990

AN "F" TRAIN FRIEND

Dear lady, paint a smile
for us please. We've all had
a long rough day and we need
your graceful cheer
to get us through
another New York City night—
a night much like other nights.
A night filled with bright lights
and fast flights.

My fine lady, lend me the time
to tell you all of the things
that are going on
in my life—all of things,
which drive me to drive—that keep me
dancing through the business mines
and booby traps, which snap
at a foot's nap
and an inch's time.

Sweet, tender lady,
thank you
for your silent recognition
and patience
on another cold New York City winter night—
a night much like other nights.
A night filled with too many
bright lights
and fast flights.

RWS
2.27.91

CENTRAL PARK...EASTSIDE

Leaves tumbling on the cobble,
spaniels tugging on the leash,
nannies pulling on the handle,
limousines floating on the street.

Artists buy some signs,
tourists buy a bye,
natives buy quality time,
while comics buy some lines.

Lovers dare their truth,
cabs flex their rubber,
buses spew their fumes,
panhandlers earn their dues.

Oak benches stand firm and new,
elms sway yet stay true,
grannies sneer at quite a few,
and traffic lights woo us through.

RWS
10.31.1991

Eight to one.
The number of cops to the one homeless man
who was screaming at the top of his lungs in Grand Central Terminal
for help at ten in the morning.
Lost?
Who?
The homeless man?
Or us?
Have we learned much of anything in the past 50 years?

Ugly conflict in such a beautiful place...
This exchange
makes me say to myself,
"We have not yet got it right."
We have so much more work to do
because locking up a shoeless
African American man who took Grand Central as his temporary home
is not the answer for all answers.

Talk can help.
Shouldn't we all talk?
Can we communicate better
than handcuffing a homeless man?
Isn't there a better way to get this right?
Reach out, talk, and help one another.
Eric Garner would still be alive if we did this.
It's much easier to do.

Cuffing this man hard
will only stop the progress
from ever beginning.
Will a jail cell help this man
understand life and how to succeed?
Or will it keep us
separate and lost?

RWS
2.28.2018

FALL VIEW

Thinking of fall days gone by.
Looking at leaves turn color
before my eyes
and drop—
piling into windrows.

Chilled air blows its sharp warnings.
Trees creak
in stretching resistance.
And squirrels dance—
treats in mouth.

Jingling laughter echoes from the streets.
Children sing in the park.
Birds chirp loudly—
though soon they say
farewell.

A jet rumbles overhead.
Splitting nature's scene.
The creaking trees speak
louder while chipmunks dash to their dens
and birds swoop for cover.

And I look up.
Offer a short, sweet goodbye to this fall day
and quietly walk away,
back to my warm place,
pen tucked in the corner of my cap.

RWS
9.20.1986

42ND STREET TO 25TH AVENUE

It's a beautiful sunny Tuesday morning and I sit
on a downtown D train to Brooklyn.
I've got a seat to myself with a railing to rest my arm by the door.
There are about 15 other people
as we head downtown past
West 4th Street to Broadway-Lafayette.
We lumber along in good 'ol reliable
NYC subway bumpy and bright fashion
with a soft spoken but pleasant and efficient conductor.
It's a nice late morning ride.

The places underground—and soon to be above ground
—define the essence of NYC.
The trains take us to work, home, on the town
and anywhere in between. To the beach,
the airport, over a river, under a river, around a bend,
and to the end of the line of many lines.
We praise the trains even though we grumble, we know
deep down that they will always come through.
They have come through
for about 115 straight years.

Through the years and decades, the NYC
that I love has a love affair with its neighborhood train station
—not true love—but reliable love.
A lasting love that is predictable—but never perfect.
It's a relationship that holds us, touches us
and even becomes a part of our lives—these trains.
Over the East River we go to Brooklyn
and leave Manhattan for a short time but
we will back to the motherland of the apple
soon.

Stalled on the bridge for a bit, we then cruise into Atlantic Avenue,
the heart of Brooklyn.
The heart of any place is a relative term since we all define
our relationships differently.
To some, we hold two corners as the heart,
a station entrance as the center or the corner store
as the place which is home—our heart.
We all want places that are close to our own hearts.
since we like to have things to hold, ties to a treasure.
A bounty to boost us.

Love is in the air on this train.
Couples smooch, singles seek mates and the rest
take stock in what they have of their own.
I enjoy seeing people together, on this ride or any other
along the way. People thrive from each other
even though we don't know each other.
We feel the energy—the spark among us and the
friendly embrace that is invisible.
As we leave 36th Street, we move down the line and
dream to ourselves and I see these dreams float within the subway car.

Back above the ground at Ninth Avenue, the doors open
and the birds say hello. We enter another part of Brooklyn, far from the
downtown. We enter someone's backyard, someone's stoop,
someone's store, someone's front door.
We would like to knock on a front door to say "hi"
because it looks inviting and it looks like home. It could be our home.
The train is delayed for "train traffic ahead" but our conductor assures us that
"We will be moving momentarily."
Sure enough...
"Fort Hamilton Parkway next; stand clear of the closing doors!"

And we move on with subway car purpose and conviction
between the homes of many as the proud train takes us there.
We have an elevated train look into

a lot of lives in these towns of Brooklyn.
Not conventional towns, but city—towns,
which are big and boxy,
brick laden and sprinkled with street trees, just enough green to
remind us of the country.
And the rows and rows of streets go by...
...to 71st Street.

We are making good time now,
in the hinterlands of Brooklyn.
A nice breeze comes through the open doors for an instant at 79th Street.
The sun shines bright,
leaving angled shadows on the floor—which move as we do.
We see nice homes at 18th Avenue as we ride on
to 25th Avenue.
And then a lady asks her neighbor, "What time is it?" "11:30." "Thank you."
Is the conversation that I hear.
A pleasant train exchange indeed.

And as we head closer to 25th Avenue,
I hear the conductor announce the stop.
We swing into the station like someone
pulling into their driveway after work.
A few of us leave the car at 11:40 AM
on this bright and sunny Tuesday morning.
We step down the steel tread stairs one by one
—capable and strong—and then on to 86th Street
to a bustling sidewalk of this
Brooklyn home town.

RWS
5.08.2018

CHAPTER FOUR

PEOPLE

THE WRITER

I read somewhere that Hemingway
would rise early to start writing
at 6 am every morning until the words ran out.
That's one fresh and full way
to produce a great product.
Putting pen to paper
and letting the juices go
until you're done for the day,
until your brain
stops sending sentences.

Until Hemingway's typewriter ran out of ribbon or
my laptop runs short of battery life.
Then, you know that you have given it your all,
without compromise.
No excuses and no regrets.
And no looking back.
Filling the pages with convincing cause and not crummy clutter.
Then, I know that I can rest easy at the end of the day
as my thoughts are inked. Raise a glass
to toast the triumph.

RWS
8.16.2014

—I tip my hat to Hemingway and all great writers...including Philip Roth,
Somerset Maugham, Sinclair Lewis, and so many others...

DAY SCHOLAR

He's got a degree in human beings.
That's all he has.
But think about it.
He knows them and he understands them.

And he can feel them.
Move them. Touch them. Love them.
He can't make great claims.
Claims to much of anything else.

Most folks don't think much of him.
But that's okay.
He's quite content.
That's because he's got a degree in human beings.

RWS
11.22.1990

PULLS AND PATTERNS

"Let's get ready for the show.
They'll be here any minute.
What do you mean you can't find the tickets?"

"I left them on top of the dresser."

"Come on, you can't decide which jacket to wear?
What's wrong with the soft—striped silk tie
with that lightly colored blue shirt?"

"Damned if I know where my loafers are."

"Let's head for the theater.
We'll meet them at our seats.
Don't call; they'll figure it out."

"I don't think that your hair looks flat."

"Come on, jump on the parkway.
We can get there five minutes faster.
Don't worry, I'll take the car in tomorrow."

"Yes, I filled it up today."

RWS
12.09.1988

ONE LIFE

The newscaster abruptly broke into my morning
today
to say that
a lady had died.

Her name was
Karen Ann Quinlan.

My spine tingled and my heart
asked why?
I honestly didn't know if she
was still alive. Oh my God...oh my...

Ten long years,
one has waned.
Ten short years,
another has grown.

One soul has faded
and another has flourished.
Life and
death.

The truth is spoken.
It is hard to accept.
I give thanks for these passing days.
And I hope that Karen Ann rests in eternal peace.

RWS
6.12.1985

(Karen Ann Quinlan died on 6.11.1985
after being in a coma for 10 years.)

ROLL START

We pulled the '56 red International dump truck,
which had been sitting for some time
in the middle of the coop driveway
with the heavy ½" metal chain.
The Massey Ferguson utility tractor pulled it up the
dusty driveway with Jay driving the Massey.
"What gear should I put it in?" Jay asked.
Dad calmly replied, "Second low."
Dad and I were in the old International...

We were determined to get it started
with a roll start.
The battery was dead and the best way
was to pull it backwards up the long driveway
to the top of Mitchell Pond Road East
then unhook the chain,
and let it roll down the hill fast,
pop the clutch
to turn the engine over to make it start.

We tried to get that old thing
started for a good hour or so—probably 10 pulls up—
until I knew every spot in the driveway where
Dad would pop the clutch in 2nd gear to get it going.
I thought that we almost had it running
once by the bottom of the driveway
in front of pen one ...
"clump de de clump de de clump de de clump"
but the start wouldn't hold.

We gave it our best try that hot, dusty
morning back in the summer of 1974
where the flies flew out of the old crank—down
windows. I loved the smell of that old truck.

I don't remember when we decided
to give up since the old International
just wouldn't hold a start.
We then guided it back into its space on the side of the driveway,
put the chain away and went into the house for lunch.

RWS
12.03.2017

WAITED SO LONG

Undaunted slave,
wipe your memories away.
Clean your bloody hands
and shower your aching body.

Touch your face
to feel your tired skin unfold.
Know that you are now
your own master.

Sweep your neatly nestled ideas
from your mind.
Send them to the mired masses
to claim and carry.

Swing your arms high
above the boys and girls
who are now on the swings,
so take them to the slide.

RWS
2.12.1990

*(Dedicated to the release of Nelson
Mandela, who was brutally imprisoned
for 27 years and was released on
2.11.1990)*

I BOUGHT YOUR MUSIC

The Journal News ad said that there would be a garage sale
on Sunday morning from 8 to 11 am.
I was looking for some used vinyl as always
as I ventured out to buy.
The ad also said that,
"I am selling the contents of the house for my dear late friend."
I guess that the quiet rainy Sunday morning
measured my mood
as I felt a distant loss to this person
who I never knew.

Her name was Val.
I found this out with the 10 albums that I bought for 10 bucks.
She wrote her name on many of the albums.
She had a nice collection of music,
many overlapping to mine.
And all of the records were greatly cared for
in the small house in which she lived.
I don't know what she did for a living,
her age when she passed away,
or if she had any family.

I sensed a bit of solitude when walking through the three downstairs' rooms
of the house. It was peaceful and yet a little sad.
Later that night
I put on a Chopin recording
and took it all in, all of its complex beauty.
I listened with my daughter, Talia.
I told Talia that it made me feel good to keep Val's music alive and play it.
It is still Val's music which I bought.
I will care for it just as she did.
Yes, today, I bought your music.

RWS
4.21.2014

WOMAN, O FEARFUL WOMAN

Take this dollar.
May it serve you well.
Let it take you through the night.
Let it make things more right.

Take this Fifth Avenue dollar.
May it serve you well.
Let it warm your cold.
Let it feed your soul.

Take this help.
May it serve you well.
Let it overshadow the passing flares.
Let it block out the blank stares.

Take my goodness.
May it serve you well.
Let it make up for the rest.
Let it heal and caress.

Take my farewell.
May it serve you well.
Let it sooth you indeed.
Let it be what you need.

RWS
11.14.1989

NEW YEAR'S NIGHT WALK

Ten degrees with a wind chill of minus three,
we set out for a
New Year's night walk,
Seth and I.
After dinner, it felt good,
the incredibly cold air
and silent steps of our boots.
We talked about wrestling the whole way.

"Let's go to Brayton and up the hill and home,"
Seth suggested.
I said, "Sure, let's go!"
I was starting to get into the stride.
The steps started getting faster and more sure,
more solid of our walk and our
destinies—as a parent who sees his nearly
18—year—old son lead the way.

We got more steps for our step counters and
more exercise for ourselves, but we also
gained a great feeling of being on top
of our game and our goals,
our respective times in this great big game of it all.
Our embracing the cold as a sign
that no element can stop us in our quest for what we
set out to conquer.

"Let's go to the mailbox at Colvin and turn around."
I suggest. Our strides were long and quick—paced and
Seth said, "Sure, that's long enough."
We touched the old blue mailbox and I said,
"Hail to old Glory!"
We then turned around
and made the return leg of the walk back
even more satisfying than the start.

RWS
1.02.2018

CHAPTER FIVE

PLACES

STAMFORD STATION

Overhead wires flap a ton of voltage
while today's news makes its way to the tracks.
Hustling commuters depart and scramble.
The day's long done on Wall Street.

People look so staid.
Few sneak a smile.
They speak few words.
They plunge ahead.

What are they looking for
in their lives?
What are they striving for
in our world?

Nobody offers a hint
of an explanation.
Seen or spoken.
And I find few answers.

So I grab my bags
and shuffle toward the incoming train.
It's right on time.
And I notice the news on the tracks tumble away.

RWS
8.01.1988

INDIANA NIGHT TRAIN

Oh, Indiana night train,
shuffling like an elephant
through the grasslands,
by and by.

You shout aloud
to warn your trespassers
louder and louder.
You sound your horn
again and again
and raise your trunk of steel
in triumphant glory,
heading for your plains' destinations.

Indiana night train,
please pass by
so your clanging bell
dwindles into gentle memories
like echoes fading
down an empty tunnel.
Soon, I'll be able
to get back to sleep.

Oh, Indiana night train,
shuffling like an elephant
through the grasslands,
by and by.

RWS
9.10.1990

WISCONSIN MORNING BLUES

Drivin' me down
you big 'ol land
of vast stillness.
Headin' south
of Tomah
I go.
Northern Wisconsin
muddy pastures
taking me down.

Yet, on the 6:45 morning road,
fond memories
keep me company.
Some rolling hills appear,
stretching the plains' backs—
flexing and twisting.
They remind me
of my Catskill
homeland.

Take me
home
rolling hills.
Take me
home ...
Goodbye
Wisconsin ...
Hello
Minnesota ...

RWS
9.11.1990

FOGGY MINNESOTA

Foggy Minnesota.
Open your eyes.
You're too beautiful
to hide under a blanket of clouds.

Come out
and greet a new day,
a new friend,
another one of your fans.

Meet your visitors.
Shake their hands,
one and all.
Don't disappoint them.

Foggy Minnesota,
where are you on this fine morning?
Why are you sleeping so late
on a Tuesday?

RWS
9.11.1990

BADLANDS SONGS

Badlands,
sing to me
all of your crooked
and crafty tunes,
you giant amusement
climbing all about.
Daring, nasty
things that you are.
Bold and real
yet you seem
so surreal.
Oh Badlands,
love your
South Dakota playground!

RWS
9.12.1990

DETROIT

Mighty memories
all but gone.
Urban prairie if ever
there was one.

Tell me where
a few hundred thousand
people
disappear?

Detroit—you can be
re—Americanized back
to the glory days of GM gold and
Buick bullishness!

But just who will get
Detroit humming again?
It's going to be the urban homesteaders
and the proud pioneers of America.

Detroit, oh Detroit.
I guess that you slipped badly.
For we know that it's been made elsewhere for a long time.
But we sense a comeback in a different way—a new way.

Forever Detroit,
you might stand on one leg but we will figure it out.
We will find a way for you to rise again above the rusted relics in your
backyard. I know that we can do it.

RWS
5.09.2013

CHAPTER SIX

SOCIETY

WINDOW WATCHER

The window watcher sees
all the days retire.
One by one.
He applauds some and
jeers others.
And the rest,
he can't quite
measure the worth.

He asks the people
who toil for five days or more
and then waste a bit.
"What do you folks know?"
"You, who are trying to become something
in this or that?"
"You, who mechanically move.
You badly need to be oiled."

"What reality do you confess?" he further begs.
"Your huge tree is dying fast.
Your abstraction masks
your daily disguise.
You're retiring the universe too soon.
And you're firing the great souls
and the great minds.
And the movements."

The window watcher
never asks these questions
to the people he watches.
He asks them to himself.
He fears the answers.
But he hopes that someday he will have the courage
to ask the questions.
And he hopes even more that
the answers will surprise him.

RWS
4.20.1982

SUPPLE AND SCRAPED

What about those
who unlike others
remain torn,
battered,
shackled—denied?

The wise know what to do.
Yes they do.
As do those who dare to ask,
but what about those
who opt for naught?

Lights illumine roads
for lucky souls
but flickering candles
can only lead
a select few clear.

And fortunate dwellers
turn themselves off, one by one,
they flicker out while mired masses
lie in the bad dreams
of a bitter reality.

RWS
3.9.1988

INVISIBLE SOCIETY

Please go away.
Bring back the people
and an easier way
for us to enjoy today.

Stop pretending that the miracles
of invisibility rival
the realities
of touching each other.

Tell us why we should
revel in the greatness
of invisibility and
technological trinkets.

Send me a message
from the invisible society to explain
this prosperity and the greatness
of sheer invisibility.

I try to reconcile
today and tomorrow
but yesterday's days
seem so much better.

Remind me why we
invented this superior way
of life and where exactly it's supposed
to lead us.

RWS
4.23.2013

BLUE

Man, it's cold on the streets of Gettysburg on a windy MLK morn.
A man shuffles up to the Lincoln Diner counter to say
that he "lost his blue canvas wallet" between
"here and the apartments a couple of blocks away."
The counterman didn't say much to the man
as he rang the loud register.
The wallet-less man left the diner
in a tired shuffle down
Carlisle Street towards the Transit Center.

"I think that he's from the shelter"
the counterman then said to our waitress.
I wonder if the counterman is right and if any
of the other dozen patrons noticed his comment at all?
This exchange that took place?
Was I the only one who heard it?
The other diners were enjoying their $6.99 breakfast specials.
Sorry to say, it does not surprise me.
I have seen this time and again.

I saw the man through the streaky diner window
head further down Carlisle in aimless, tentative steps.
I know that type of step. I have seen it all too many times.
Too many to count.
It's something that I wish I didn't notice at times
and wish I didn't take on the duty to wonder how this man
will get by on this very cold day?
Does he really have a place today
or even when the skies are warm and sunny?

It is a painful picture to see and it can hit you hard.
Especially, when I comfortably sit on a full wallet
and have a firm direction to go.
That shaky step is not always visible.

But one day when you see it,
you will know clear as can be.
I hope that you look up from your breakfast special for a moment.
Even though it will make you
kind of blue.

RWS
1.20.2014

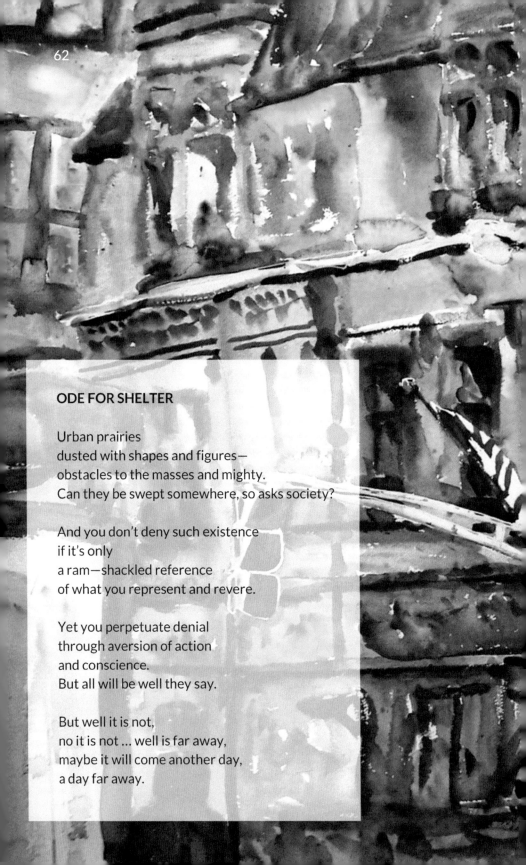

ODE FOR SHELTER

Urban prairies
dusted with shapes and figures—
obstacles to the masses and mighty.
Can they be swept somewhere, so asks society?

And you don't deny such existence
if it's only
a ram—shackled reference
of what you represent and revere.

Yet you perpetuate denial
through aversion of action
and conscience.
But all will be well they say.

But well it is not,
no it is not ... well is far away,
maybe it will come another day,
a day far away.

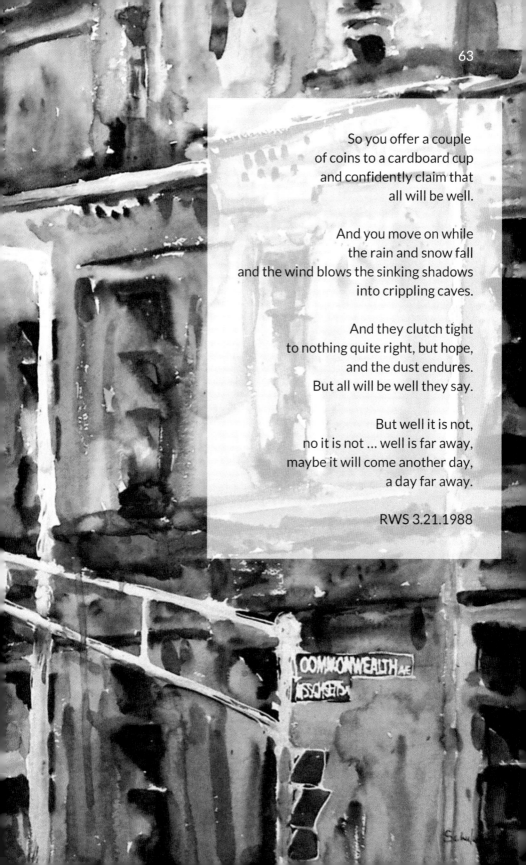

So you offer a couple
of coins to a cardboard cup
and confidently claim that
all will be well.

And you move on while
the rain and snow fall
and the wind blows the sinking shadows
into crippling caves.

And they clutch tight
to nothing quite right, but hope,
and the dust endures.
But all will be well they say.

But well it is not,
no it is not ... well is far away,
maybe it will come another day,
a day far away.

RWS 3.21.1988

BENCHED

A man sits on a park bench in a very small park indeed.
Off the main drag.
Down and out and nowhere to go.
Nowhere to hide.
No shelter waiting.
No one stops to offer much of this or that.
And I think how bad will it be this winter?
I really don't want to know the answer.

It's a tale that we have heard and seen
and heard and seen again.
It is a tale that needs an end.
A happy end for a change.
Why do we live this way when so many are alone,
weathered, and worn with no purpose?
No plan.
No home.

Look around you if you dare
and see what our imperfections
have produced.
Can it be any bleaker?
Cardboard shelter and blankets as roofs.
Shopping carts as moving trucks and winter clothes in warm weather.
Shivering inside.
Warm hearts seeking a place while cold hearts walk by.

Many of us try to tend to these souls.
Make a permanent transition from a bench to a home.
A cold cardboard box to a heated apartment.
Running up against time and the cold, we build a bridge
that will take people to a safer side of life.
A better place.
Lend a hand and deliver on your plan.
Then, many living souls won't have to stay benched.

RWS
11.16.2013

UNIVERSAL

To one point in the horizon,
we gather our belongings
and sail off for the sun.
We leave the rest behind and take
a first class seat in a first rate
accommodation that we adore.

We leave the others behind for
they need not know where we
steal away.
To the sun.
Where the warmth and energy of all people collect.
To be one.

One, by the way,
and not two.
For this society is one.
For those who love being one…
"One for the books!"
I say.

It doesn't make a difference to me since
I will stay behind and enjoy the labors
of love and community.
For one, to me,
is not the ideal way.
One is just not the way.

Serve others
to release the number one idea, and then
we will all become one.
One, as a universal being,
we will see that we can truly
become one.

One is not actually one.
It is a collection of
many becoming one.
It is a formula
that we have
to add to become one.

It is universal.
Together
as
one.
Yes.
It is universal.

RWS
12.14.2013

CHAPTER SEVEN

HEART AND EMOTION

IN TUNE

Touched.
Propulsion presented
the best of
human potential.

Vibrated.
Chances collided
and expanded breaths
arose front and center.

Aflood.
Answers awoke
this being and
this spirit of realization.

Danced.
I grabbed
a new wave or two,
didn't I?

RWS
5.03.1988

FORWARD EYES

Cast no aspersions
on those rain—swept plans,
which get flung into the wind.
Only to evaporate.

Lift your head above
these storms
and take a slow look
around.

Save your eyes
from teardrops.
They sprinkle the ground.
They show your soft side.

Take time to break the molds
that you firmly cast,
those bowling pins, which
refuse to fall.

Touch your new reality and
leave your old box of troubles
tucked in the drawer.
And off the paper.

RWS
5.23.1989

AIMING

A web unspun,
a song to be sung,
teetering and undone,
we strive to become one.

Trying to weave
more than others can believe,
our demands tear and cleave
and we regretfully leave.

Alone and apart,
we shed skins of the heart,
and I long to throw
another dart.

RWS
4.29.1990

CAUGHT

Sneaking up like the tide—
the way that it brushes seaweed
into crooked windows
on the morning shore.

> I didn't see it coming.
> I wonder if people ever see it at all.

It finally seemed that my time
had arrived.
One's moment of truth
ripening under the sun.

> Our senses and feelings woven together.
> But not for real.

The times became
another blind vision, a dead-end road.
Trying to take me to places,
which I can't quite imagine.

> But places that I dearly
> would like to see.

RWS
11.08.1989

ENTANGLEMENT

Nearly spent
my last dime
of memory
on your thoughts today.

Clearly believed
that I had used
my precious energy
as I sunk deep.

Surely caught,
my heart tripped
on the line
of falling down.

Calmly whispered
a familiar jest
as I stepped around
the swirling storms.

RWS
6.10.1985

AUGUST WIND

The sands of the shore
dribbling lessons of love
through the rippling waves.
Her body of movement
sends the tide crashing
into my soul.

Splashing thoughts
through the water
brings seeming conclusions.
So right.
It belongs to the future
of what's here tonight.

RWS
8.03.1991

A WRITER'S SKETCH

Tonight, I draw myself for you.
Sketching the outline, shading the background,
coloring the body,
painting the picture.
I deliver myself unedited.

Perhaps you're not ready for this complete picture.
Not ready, yet, to hold it to you.
Standing alone and independent seems so inviting.
You long for diversity and challenge.
You listen to my offer of compromise.

You're an artist; perhaps you understand
compromises well. Perhaps you don't.
Your canvas of paintings depicts similar images.
Like thoughts.
Arrowed conviction.

I'm a writer.
I deliver through my pen.
I long to tell you how I became inspired by you.
But I'll let you read
my message instead.

I love your wit and intelligence.
It's reflected in your persona and your painting.
You stand tall, speak firmly, and reach for a lot.
You reach for it all.
You want to see more.

And I do too.
There's so much more that I want to see and do.
Have to see and do.
Alone and apart.
Two and together.

You might not see my yearnings all so closely.
But they are there.
Your's might seem too inviting but
mine remain there for the taking.
And for the taking I will offer.

I stand before you with no promise.
No guarantee.
I release my sketch to you to view.
To see a deeper image
of the same goofy clown and tender loving soul.

Take a closer look.
For yourself.
Carry this picture with you.
Pull it out when you feel.
Place it where you wish.

RWS
11.24.1991

CHAPTER EIGHT

GETTING AHEAD

MOUNTAIN WALK

Stretching to find.
Forgetting to think.
Reading the map.
Leaving the road.

Climbing to see.
Closing my eyes.
Lifting my pride.
Seeing new sides.

RWS
9.14.1990

SEPTEMBER WISDOM

That moment
when the September sun reassured me
and the September wind cleared me
is when I stopped to see time,
second by second,
step before me.

I sat on the edge of the garden
in what appeared to be
the edge of my mind.
Tired and tender
from mounds of exhaustion.
Years of toil.

I saw the past Septembers
in all their magnificent change
suddenly greet me.
All twenty-eight.
Different though they were,
They brought one message, "We don't change."

With this before me,
I felt compelled to respond.
"Yes, we do change," I said
to myself and to all those Septembers.
They just stood there and listened.
I knew that they wouldn't respond.

And I didn't look for a response.
The answers were before me.
The seasons change and years age us.
The leaves fall and the greens rest.
And the more things seem to change,
the more that they remain the same, we remain the same.

I feel wiser for this encounter, a bit broader.
Feeling the September sun reassure me
and the September wind clear me.
It's when I stopped to realize how we and time
grow together, yet not anew.
I realized this at that moment.

RWS
9.21.1991

THE BEAUTY OF THIS MOMENT

Seeing the clearness of this moment
before me,
reminds me to count every minute of every day
like precious jewels.
Prized possessions.
Irreplaceable moments in our lives.

Time never repeats; life's record never skips.
Never has and never will.
Make the most of this moment.
Right now and tomorrow too.
Love the beauty and give thanks for the goodness.
And the abundance.

Give thanks for being able
to do anything,
realizing that we live
and grow
every minute
of every day.

Yes, there are ups and downs,
Frowns, clowns and out of towns, betwixed and betweens,
and sometimes people are just mean.
But yet goodness will still come through, because
it is our glue, our cue to a new thing or two.
…Things to change in me and you.

It's a long way up and a short way down.
Down with a sound that won't break the ground
but will bruise an ego or two.
We stand and shiver
but are not too weak to deliver
what we need to do to grow.

And we see again that there is beauty in all,
never too far from our fall.
In fact, when we change
and learn to bend a bit
is when we can stop and sit.
Ponder, think, and let an idea get lit.

For we will mend
and we will tend
to the frayed ends
that are in our care,
in our midst and
within our trust.

Our trust
is truly a must.
A must for you and me
and all to see.
It's a very big part in
the beauty of this moment.

RWS
11.04.2013

TOTAL VISION

Life's complete look.
The complete vantage point.
Total vision.

Complete when you realize that
all aspects of your existence
are one.

One, since the pieces interlock,
no slack at all and no leftovers either.
Total vision.

Feeling there is nothing
that can break you down.
You are completely one.

Taking on the world
one day at a time.
In perfect rhyme—no wavering at all.

Realizing that you are now
the completely developed being.
Total vision.

Eternity is yours'.
It's your journey that's
picking up a head of steam.

Enjoy the days and reel in the goodness
in all that there is for us.
Total vision.

RWS
5.30.2013

CHAPTER NINE

ALL PURPOSE POETRY

CLOUDS

Allusion is
alone
when days are of the choosing
to make.
Then the sky falls
down upon you.

RWS
4.24.1984

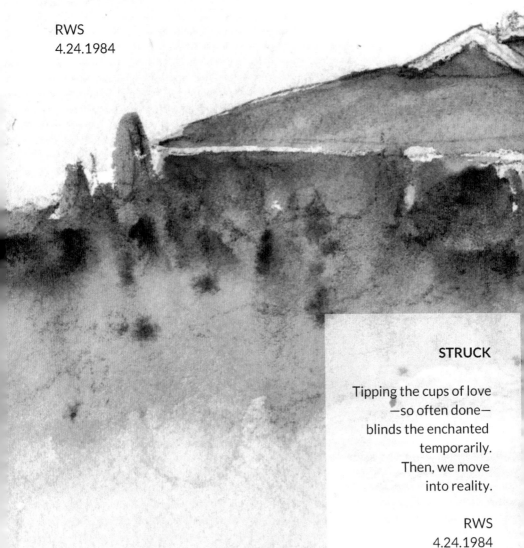

STRUCK

Tipping the cups of love
—so often done—
blinds the enchanted
temporarily.
Then, we move
into reality.

RWS
4.24.1984

A SILENCE SPEAKS

Camping in a hut
along nature's trail
of things and thoughts.
Encountering bits and pieces
of sporadic dreams.
A little here and a little there.
A lot in all.

Swaying in a hammock.
Time and occurrence sift through my space.
Fantasy and reality
clash over and again.
Making counteroffers.
Amidst it all,
My silence reaches rational conclusions.

RWS
12.06.1988

SECONDS

Our interval life maps
get stitched together
by select seconds that matter.
Matter in the sense
when we can thread the eye
of a needle's time together
in one tiny—but—connected fabric.
Our map.
It's just for us.

There is never a doubt
that we
sew the seconds of the complete
blanket of ourselves,
tucked underneath the umbrella of
wonderings, meanderings,
and purpose.
We continue
and the seconds guide us.

We question
what our next move is as
we turn back time to synchronize those
pages to the present.
It's life as one.
One through our existence
and centuries' long span
in a world of so many other seconds
that don't interfere with our plan.

The tenacity that
it takes to behold seconds
is the benefit
of it all.
All of what it means to continue
our purpose and passion of time—
strength and conviction that remains
true to the seconds that matter.
And our map continues...with these seconds.

RWS
11.23.2017

LOVE'S UMBRELLA

Love does conquer fear by a landslide.
Through the ages, lifting the goodness
in all of our hearts
above the clutter
and fear in our heads.
It's a great recipe for life.

How in the world did it take us so long to let
this sink in,
to mesh into our operating systems?
A new dawn appeared
and we landed on a different planet.
Thank goodness for that landing.

Let love be the umbrella
that covers us, protects us,
guides us, calms us,
and most importantly,
sets us on our true path of goodness
each step of the way.

RWS
1.29.2018

CHAPTER TEN

LOOKING BACK

PLAYGROUND PURITY

Kid in a basket
of trouble,
take another
fair swing.

Stop riddling
your friends
and taking
their toys.

Climb the pole
with zest
and zeal
and make your deal.

Don't cry
over the skinned knee
that you got
sliding into third.

Hike the pigskin
and block
the charging
toughs.

Sail over
the leapfroggers
and the king of the mountaineers
to claim your spot on the hill.

Let go
of the monkey bars
that are now too small
to hang from.

RWS
5.18.1990

SPIRAL TWIST

By now,
looking back at time
should resemble the joy
of turning the pages
of your favorite photo album,
which gladly accepts
being taken
from its snug spot on the shelf.

Blowing dust off time.
Rewinding the recorded tapes in your head.
Holding a few frames in place for a second look.

But time
plays tricks,
and feelings mature.
Memories
turn
into sinking sliders.
And they're too damn hard
to hit.

RWS
1.31.1988

MY 1968 EYES

A dynasty of books captivates
my five—year—old eyes
which gawk from below, while
a grandfather clock boasts
endless motion, pendulum in its gullet.

> And the wood floor
> leaks occasional creaks.

A flock of chickadees chat
about the weather outside
the kitchen window, while
a round old radio spews the late 1960's not so good news
to a tray of freshly baked goodies.

> And the mail huddles
> the blue countertop.

A porch screen door opens
the invitation
to one and all, while
a gentle grandmother introduces the savory servings
to the hungry appetites' delight.

> And my eyes tingle through the rays
> of the scattered spring sun.

RWS
4.21.1982

NO JOKE

I was reading in the living room,
sipping a new red wine that I had no idea if I liked yet.
But it grew on me.
In fact, it tasted pretty damn good after the first half glass.
I liked it and it bathed the moment.

After taking another sip, an old song came off the vinyl
and it took me back. Way, way back.
To a time where innocence overruled reality
and dreams never ran away. It was a time of
crystal blue skies and no rain at all.

A couple of tears greeted the middle of the second stanza of this song.
I didn't see this coming and couldn't stop missing that time,
the rambunctious childhood, even for one look back.
The time that is preserved like a fossil, which
I can clearly recall.

Taking it in, remembering the times running on the lawn,
playing games until dark. Sweaty and tired and full of life
with not a worry in the world. It was a time. Funny how
a simple three minutes of verse transports you back 45 years
to years of joy. It's truly a wonder. And it's no joke.

RWS
9.18.2013

COUNTING

I sit alone in the kitchen on a beautiful Sunday morning,
reading the latest New Yorker.
I pause to hear the kitchen clock.
Ticking.
Louder as I listen, silent as I read, muted as I sip my coffee.
Changing volumes in my mind,
this clock has been a part of my life for
forty—one years.
Hopefully, for forty or fifty more.

Ticking away the days.
Every day, rain or shine.
Hot or cold,
it leads the way.
Second by second,
only to be glanced at
a couple of times a day.
Secure in the corner, hung on the wall,
providing comfort.

"So clock on the wall,
how am I doing after
all these years?
Tell me what the future holds.
You have been with me almost my whole life.
I'd love to know if a timepiece knows.
What comes next?"
Counting away.
So slow.

I return to my article
and sip my coffee.
Not hearing a sound,
yet, the clock guides
me through the days and
now the decades.
I was nine when this clock arrived.
I am now
fifty.

I guess that everyone needs an anchor
in their lives,
a tangible fort.
Whatever gets the job done.
I then turn from page 82 to page 83.
I don't hear a sound until
I lift my head from the very well written page and turn to look
at the clock, which is still patiently and firmly
counting.

RWS
9.07.2013

RECONNECT

Stepping forward in time
to reconnect to the past.
How we long to relive
some safe and secure days
of our innocence
and shall I say,
our brilliance.

We look forward every day,
yet we look over our shoulder
now and then
to pull the past
front and center
in line
with our footsteps today.

Like it or not,
tomorrow's history
is not known nor
is the day after.
But, we can look forward
to reach back and harvest
a glow.

I know that it's not a great game
to play too often,
but it is a reliable pastime
to think about it.
Take a pause,
breathe deeply, reach back
and reconnect.

RWS
11.01.2017

ABOUT THE AUTHOR, RONALD W. SCHULMAN

Ron Schulman grew up in the Sullivan County Catskill Mountains of New York where he was born in December 1962. He is a graduate of Hunter College, the City University of New York, where he holds a BA in Urban Affairs and an MUP in Urban Planning. He owns his own affordable housing development firm. Ron has been writing poetry for the past 40 years ever since 11th grade as this is one of his favorite pastimes. He sees the world unfiltered; he listens as he walks, never with ear buds or headphones. He enjoys the sounds of nature and of people as they walk through their lives. Ron has built affordable housing for people who have difficulty finding decent places to live. His poetry compliments this work as he speaks about the human condition and what we need to do to help heal this world.

Ron lives in Scarsdale, NY, just 25 miles north of midtown Manhattan with his wife Miriam, and his grown children, Talia and Seth, who are both presently in college. In addition to poetry, he enjoys reading, yoga, Pilates, great red wine, and his vinyl record collection, which is approaching 2,000 albums. "Music should be listened to in the best format offered, not for muted convenience," Ron offers. But to be fair to today's society, he did have the first SONY Walkman that came out in 1981; but that phase only lasted about two years!

ABOUT THE ARTIST, MIRIAM SCHULMAN

Miriam Schulman, a watercolor and mixed media artist for over 20 years is founder of the Inspiration Place, an online art class site. Schulman abandoned a hedge fund career after witnessing the devastation of 911 to work on her art full time. Rejecting the starving artist myth, her watercolor and mixed media paintings have been seen on NBC, published in art magazines & home decor books and collected worldwide.

In addition, New York museums have carried her artistic accessories in their gift shops. She has been published in art magazines such as Art of Man, Art Journaling Magazine by Stampington and was a regular contributor to Professional Artist magazine. She is a host of her own podcast, The Inspiration Place, a podcast for art lovers who want to quiet their inner critic and reconnect with their lost creativity. Listen on schulmanart.com/itunes

All art in this book is available for collecting and licensing. To inquire, email Miriam@SchulmanArt.com or visit Art.SchulmanArt.com

URGENT BEG AND PLEAD!

Thank you for reading my book!

I really appreciate all your feedback, and I love hearing what you have to say. I need your input to make the next version of this book or future books better. Please leave a helpful review on Amazon letting us know what you thought of the book.

Thanks so much,
Ron Schulman

53271111R00069

Made in the USA
Lexington, KY
28 September 2019